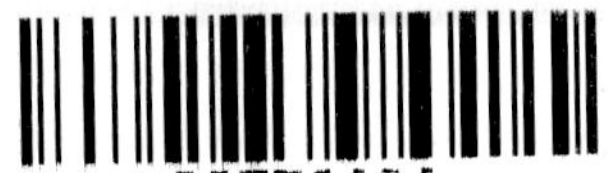

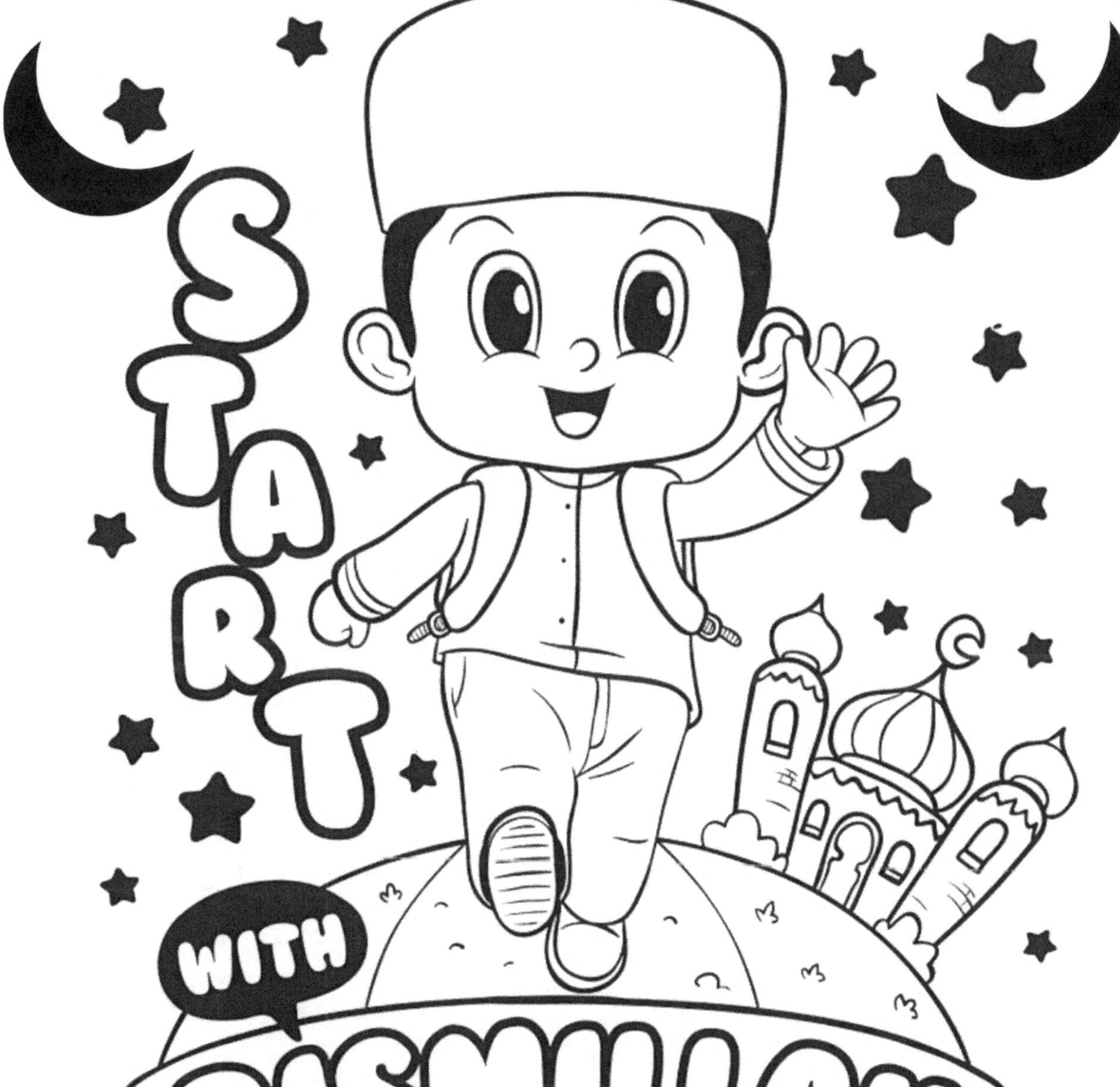

START WITH BISMILLAH

THIS BOOK BELONG TO....

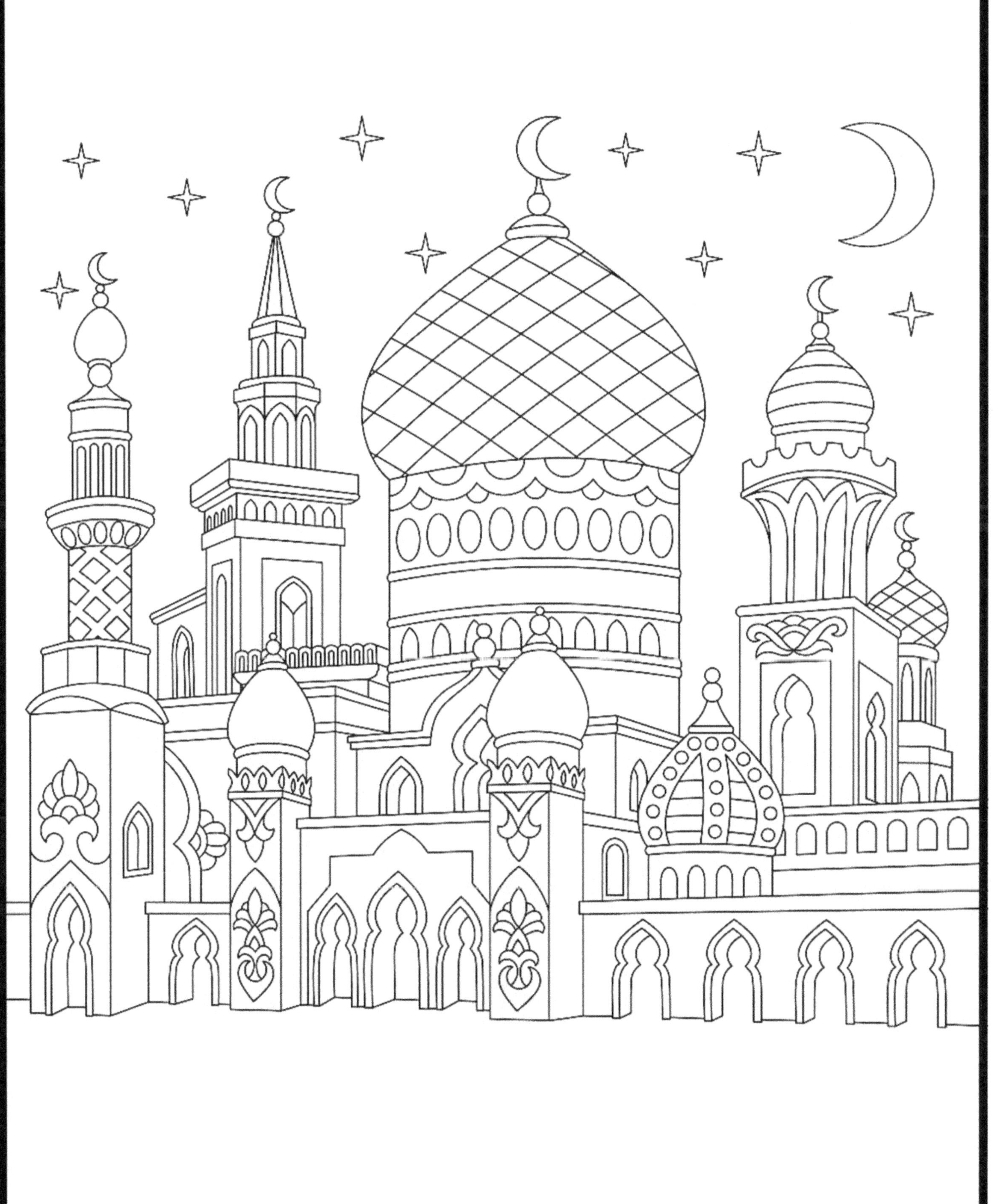

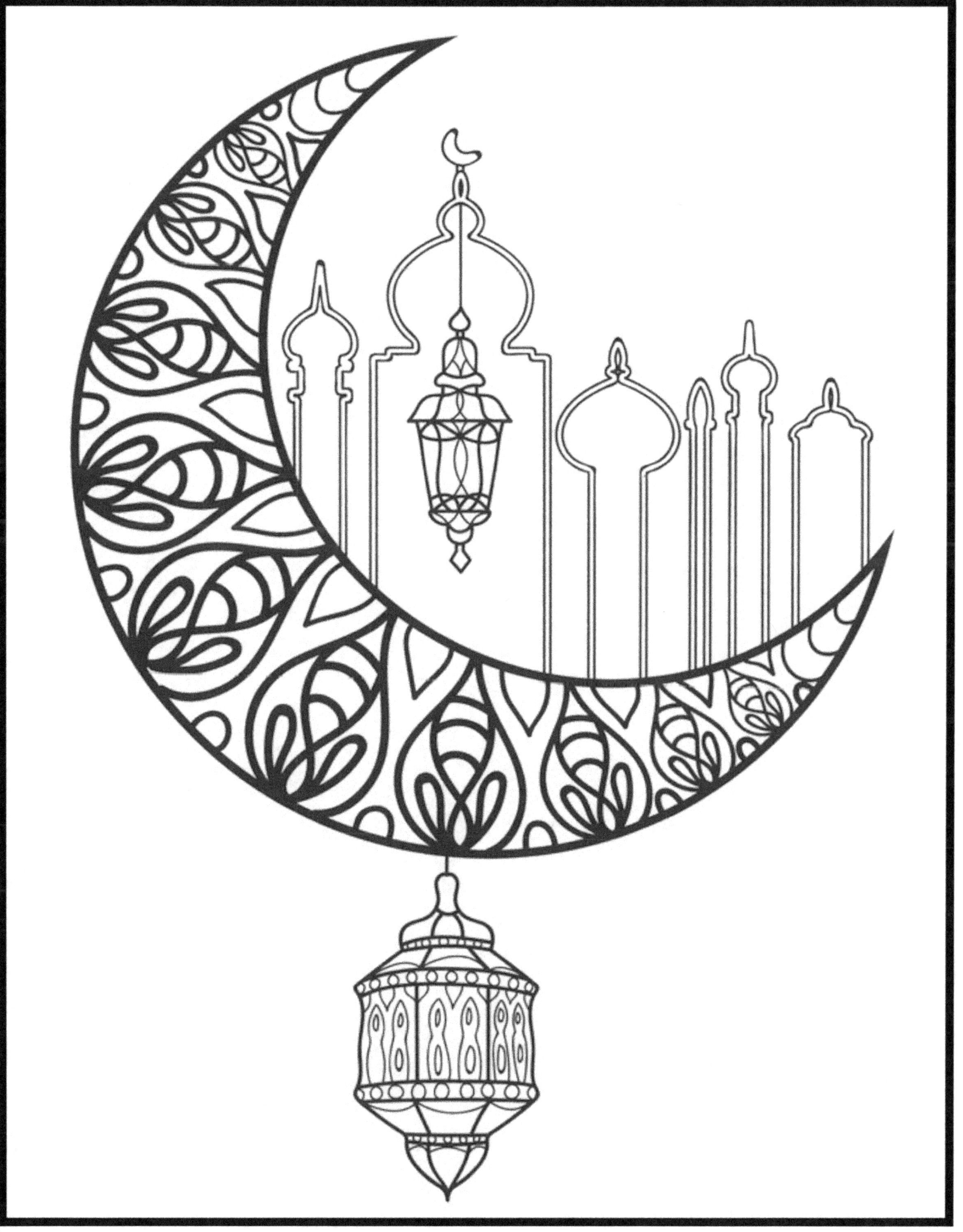

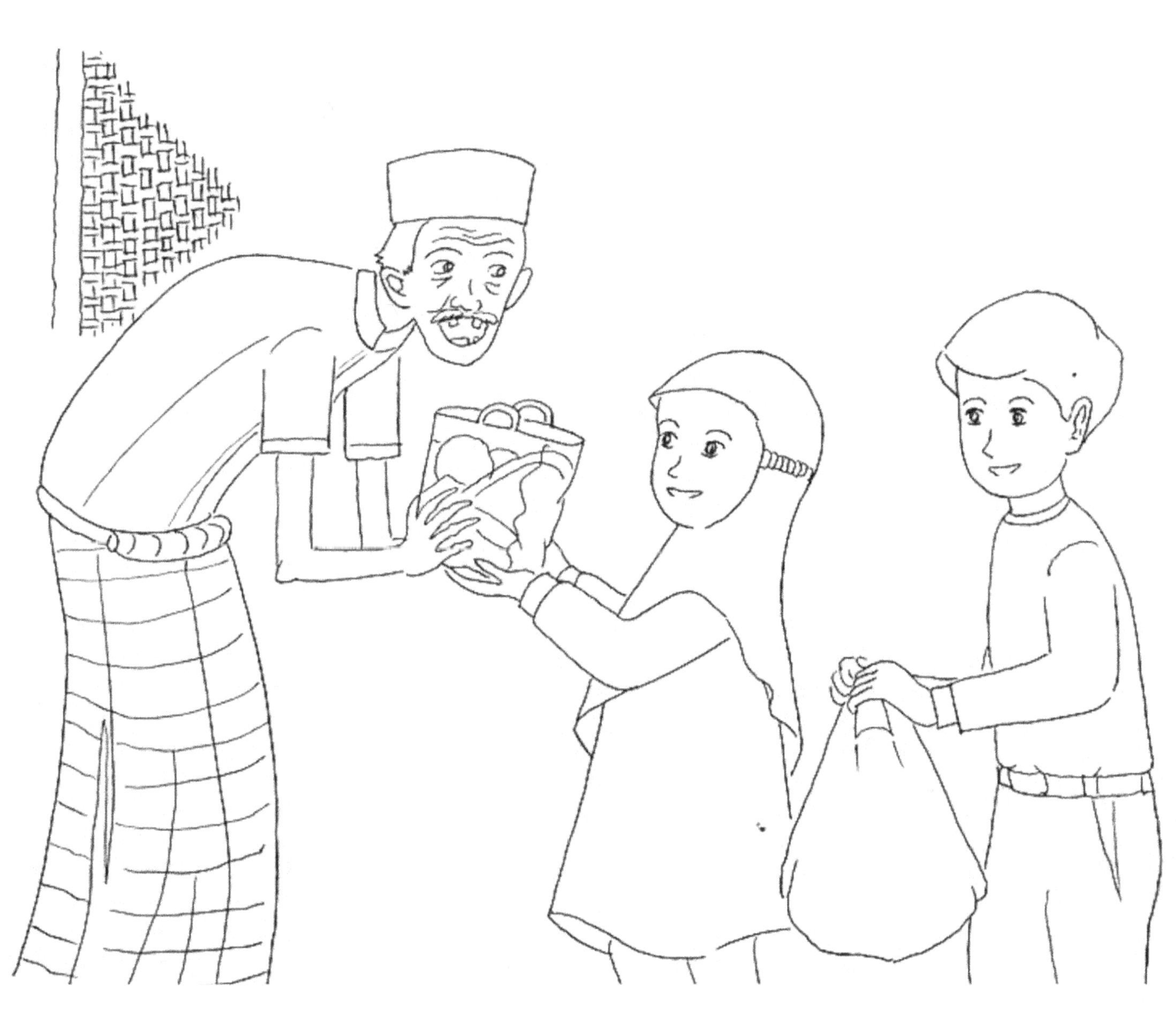

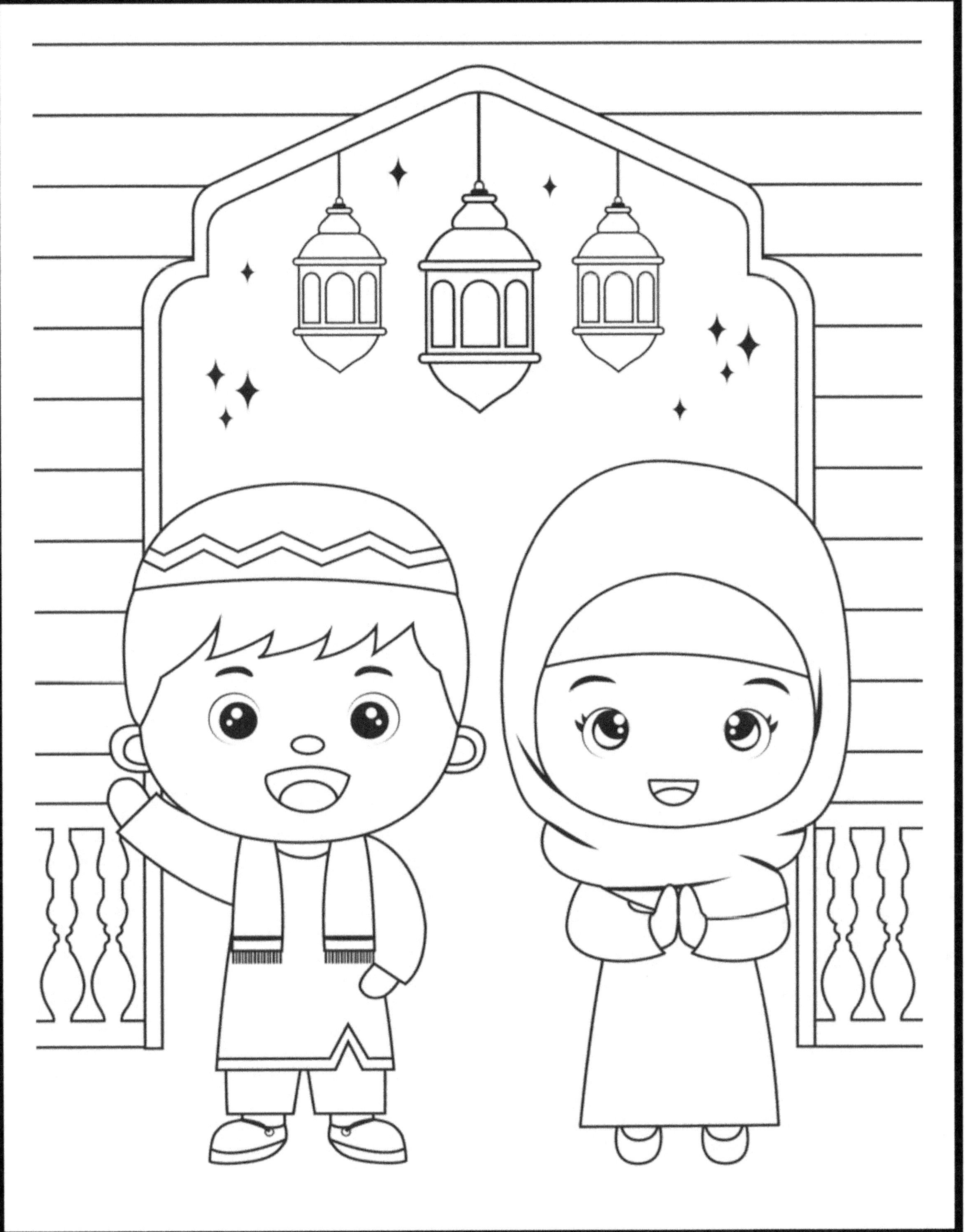

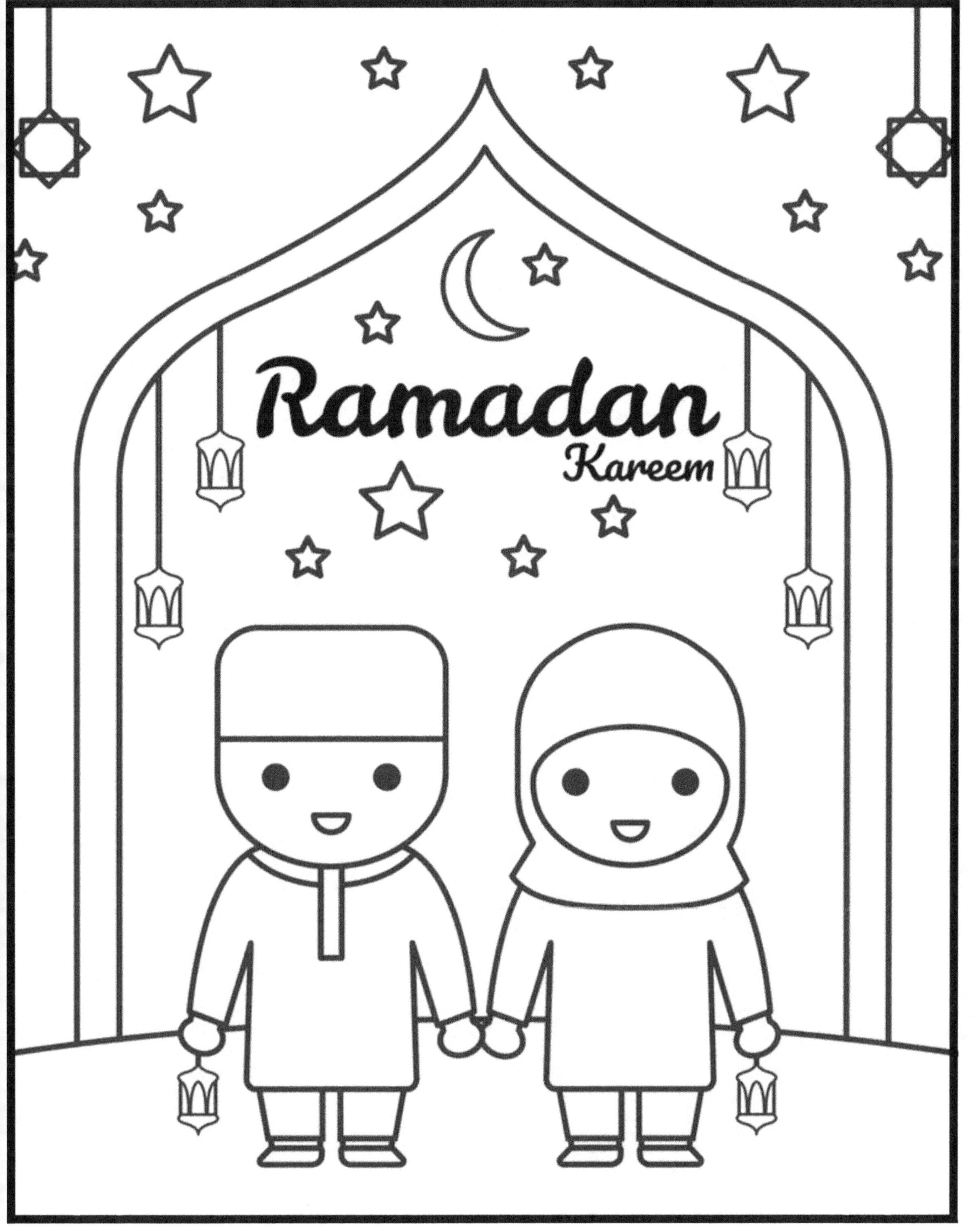

Ramadan
Kareem

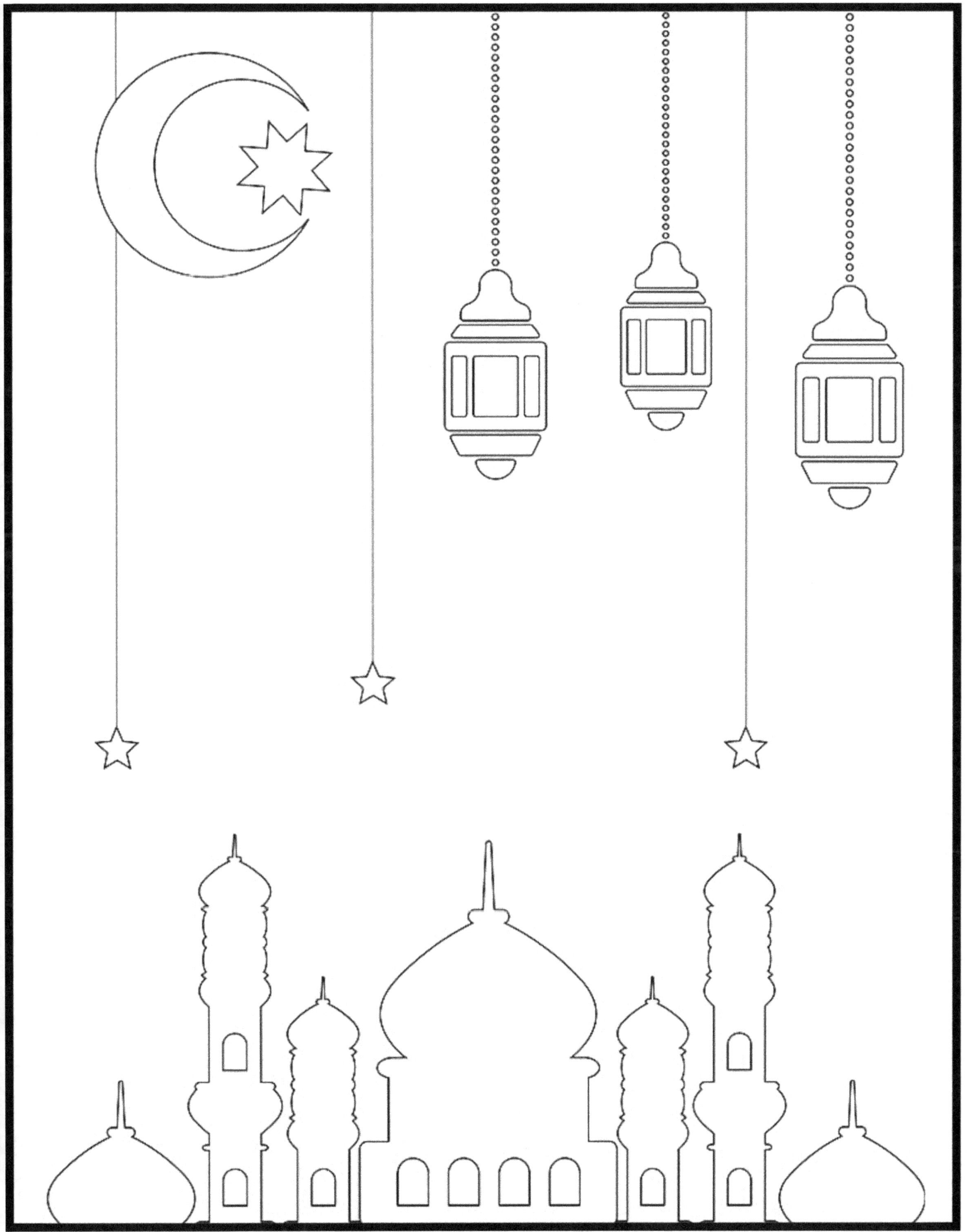

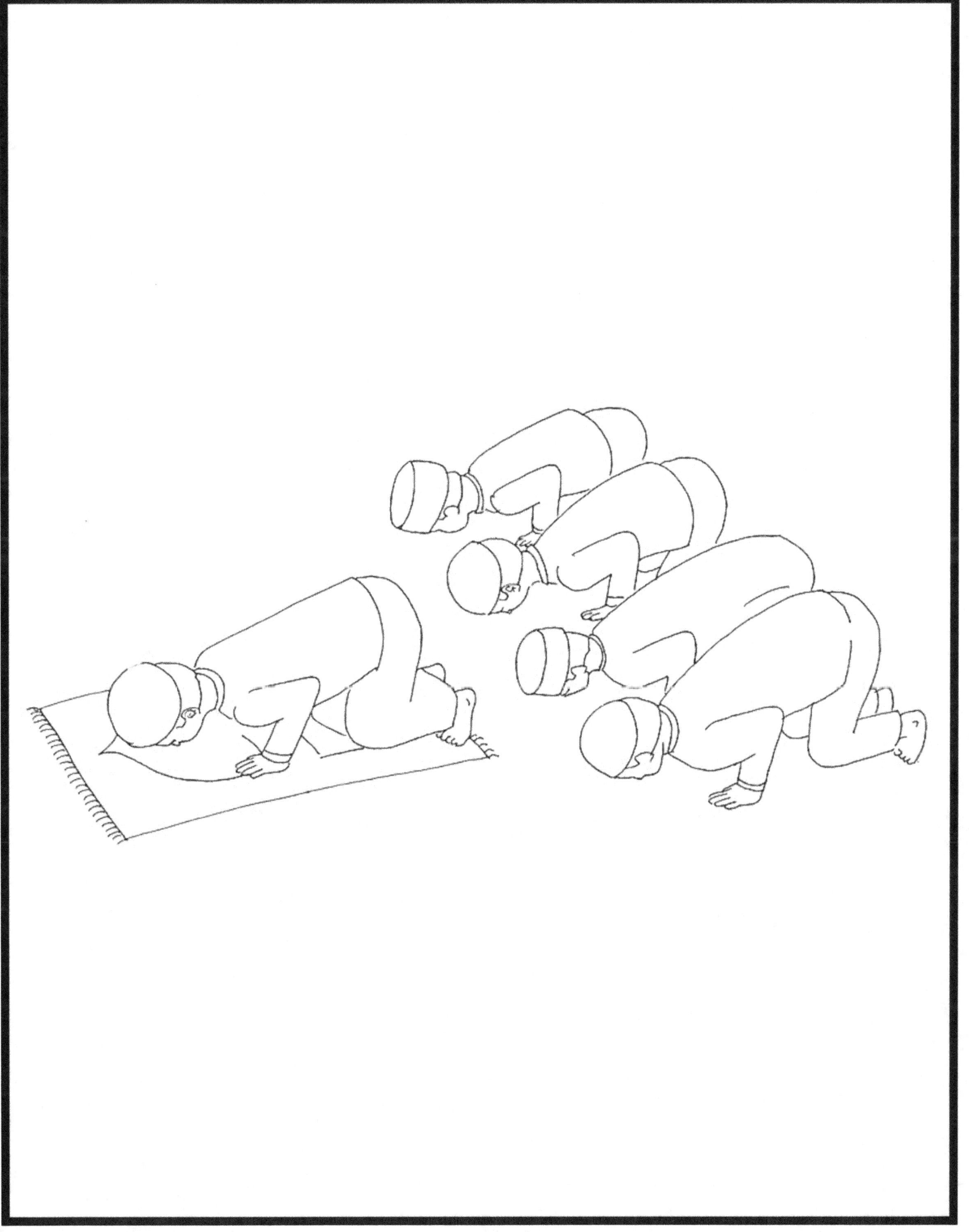

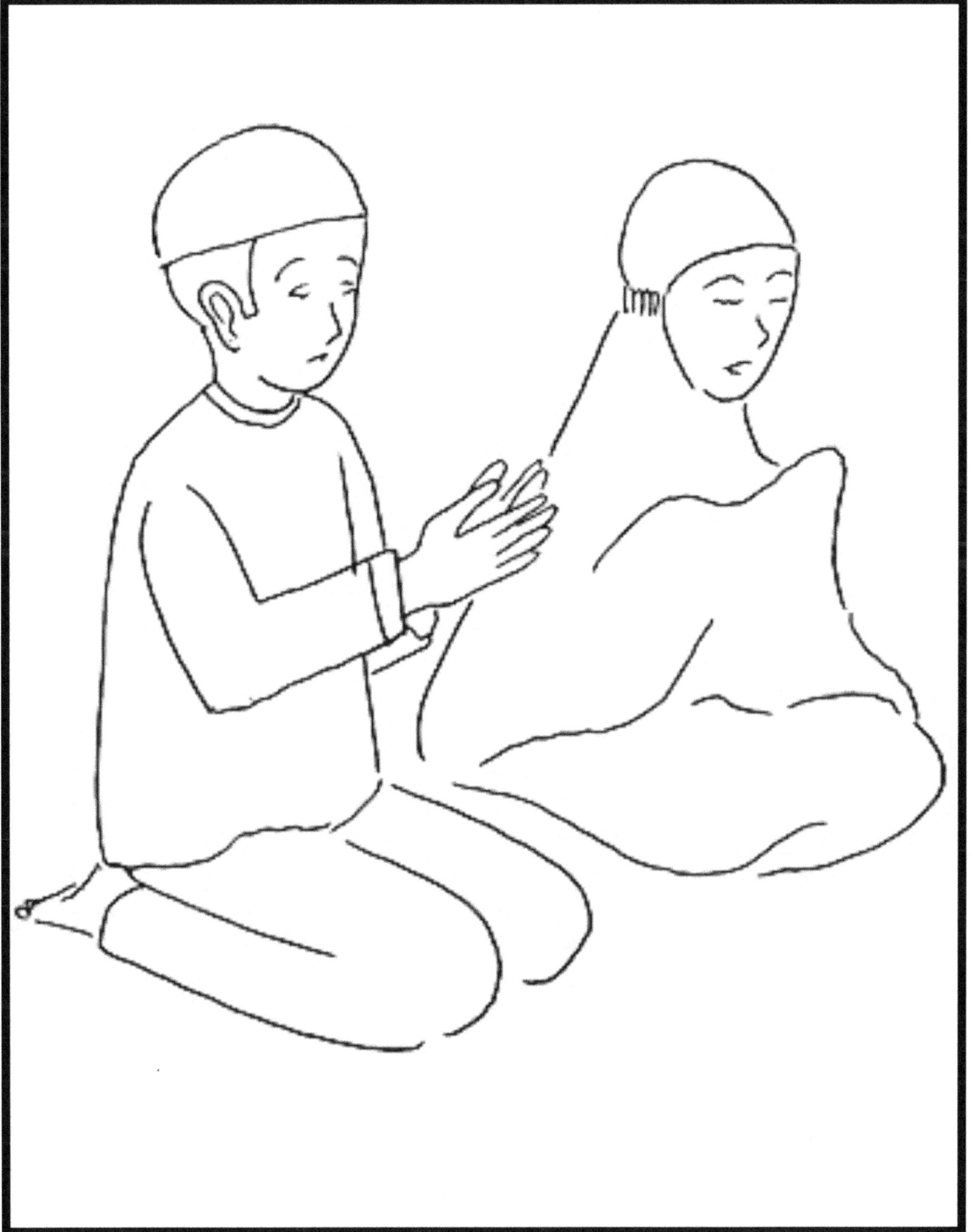

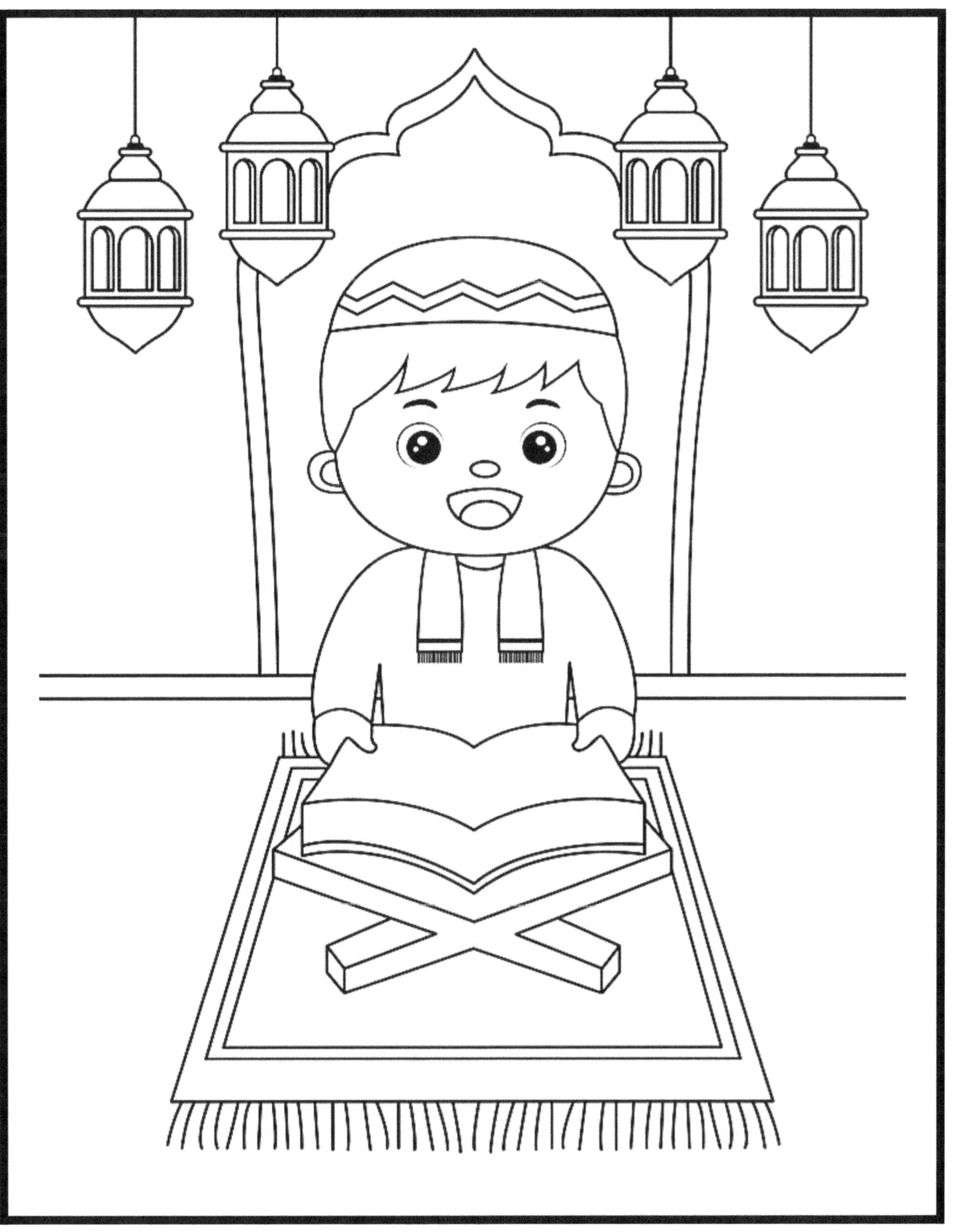

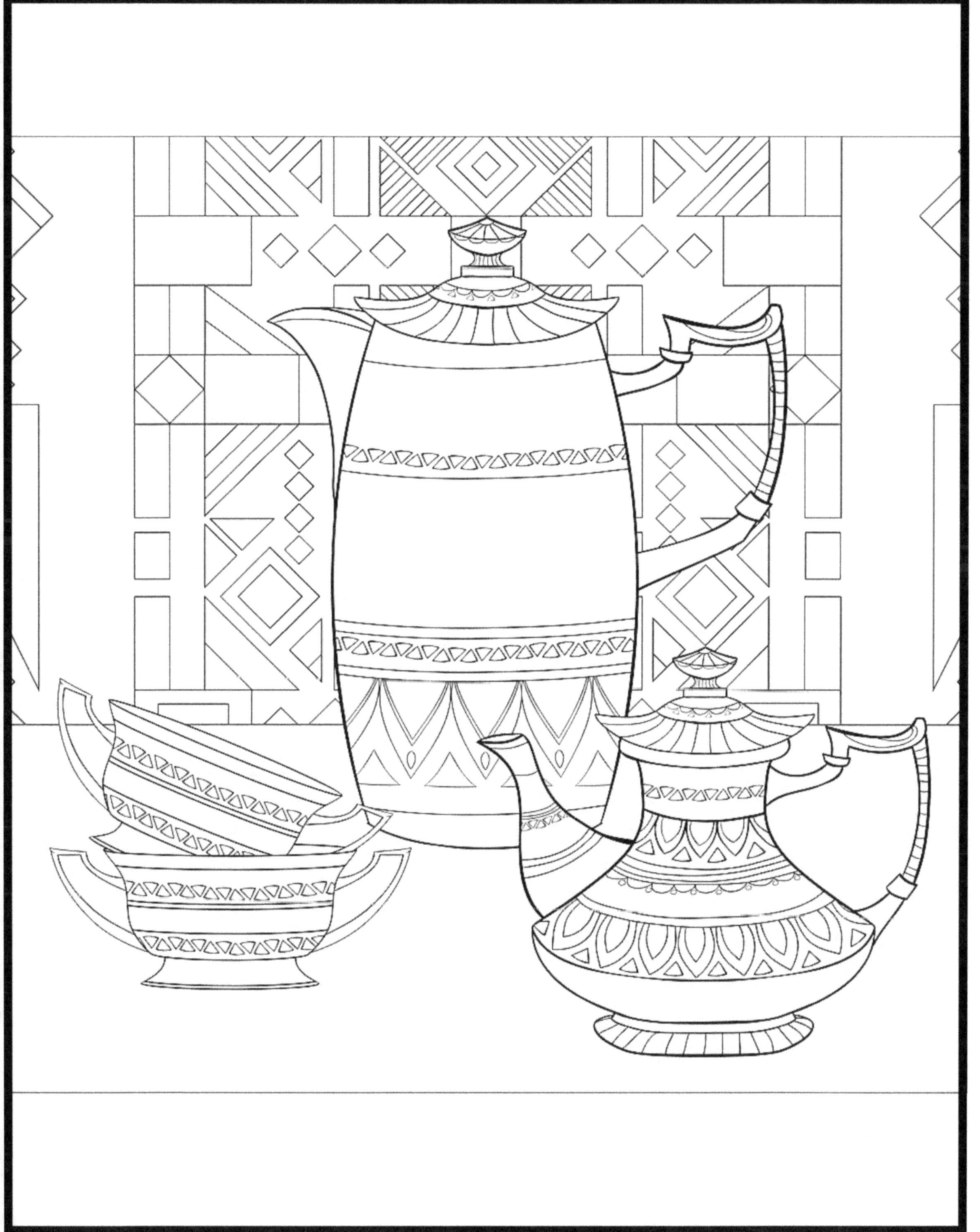

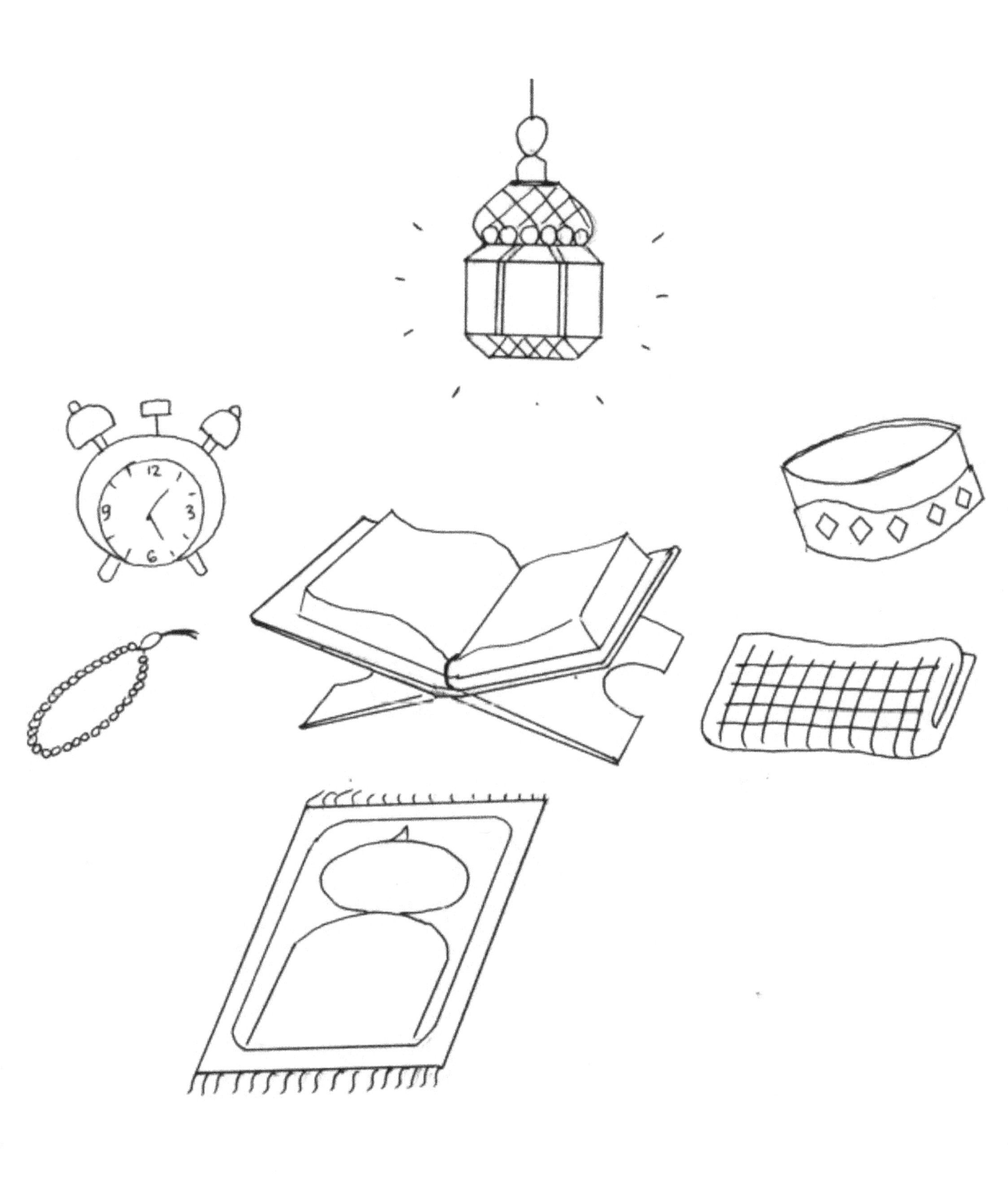

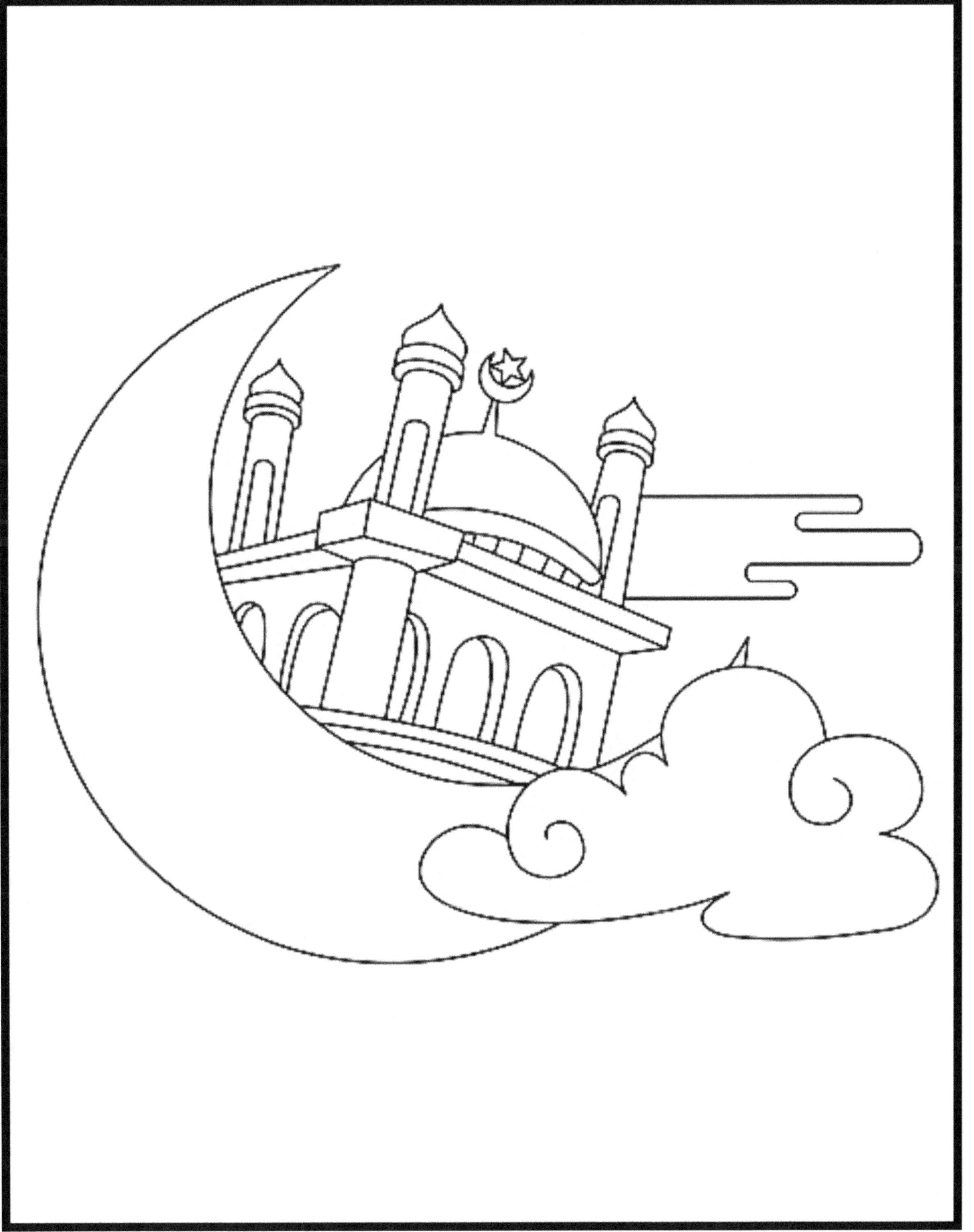

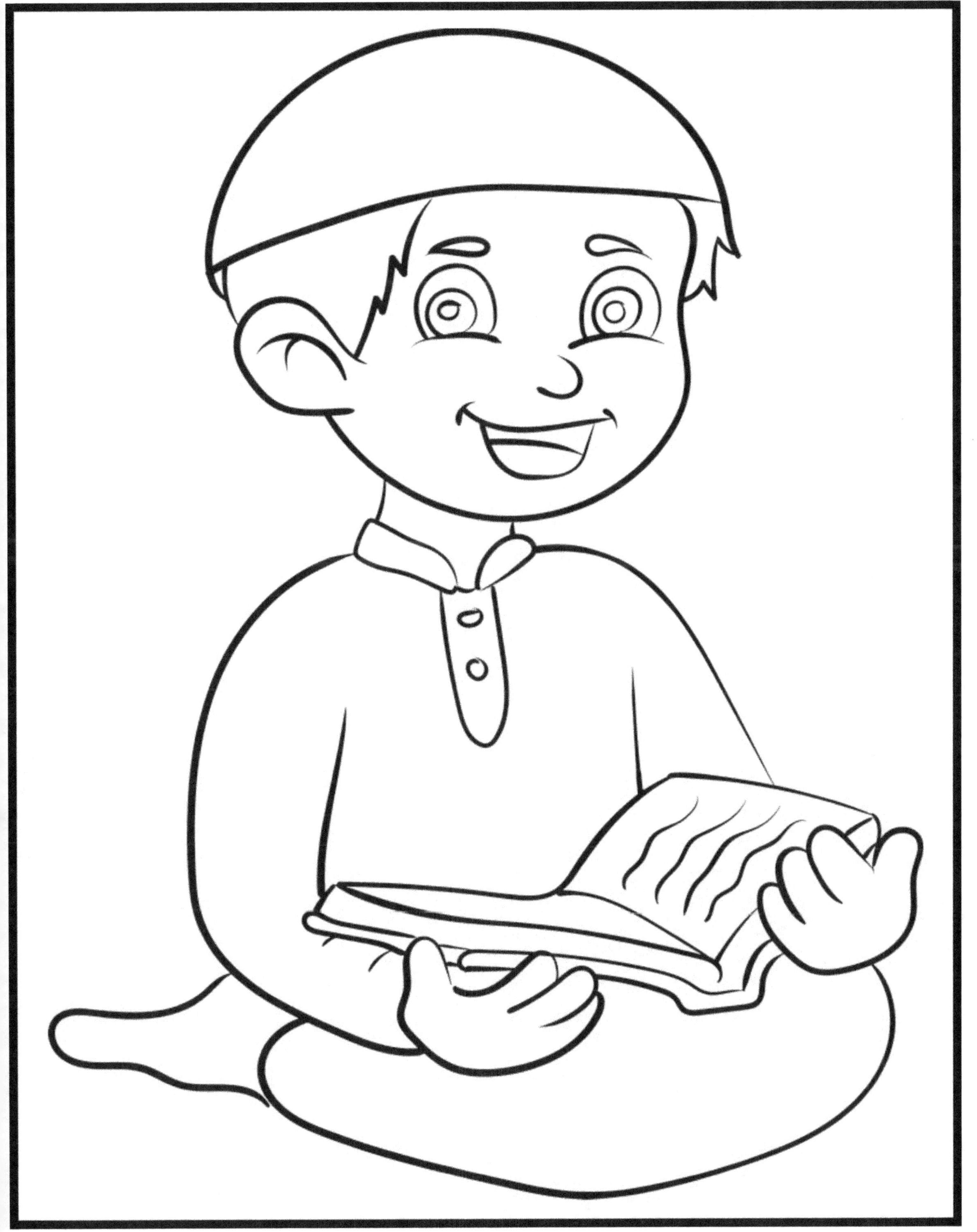

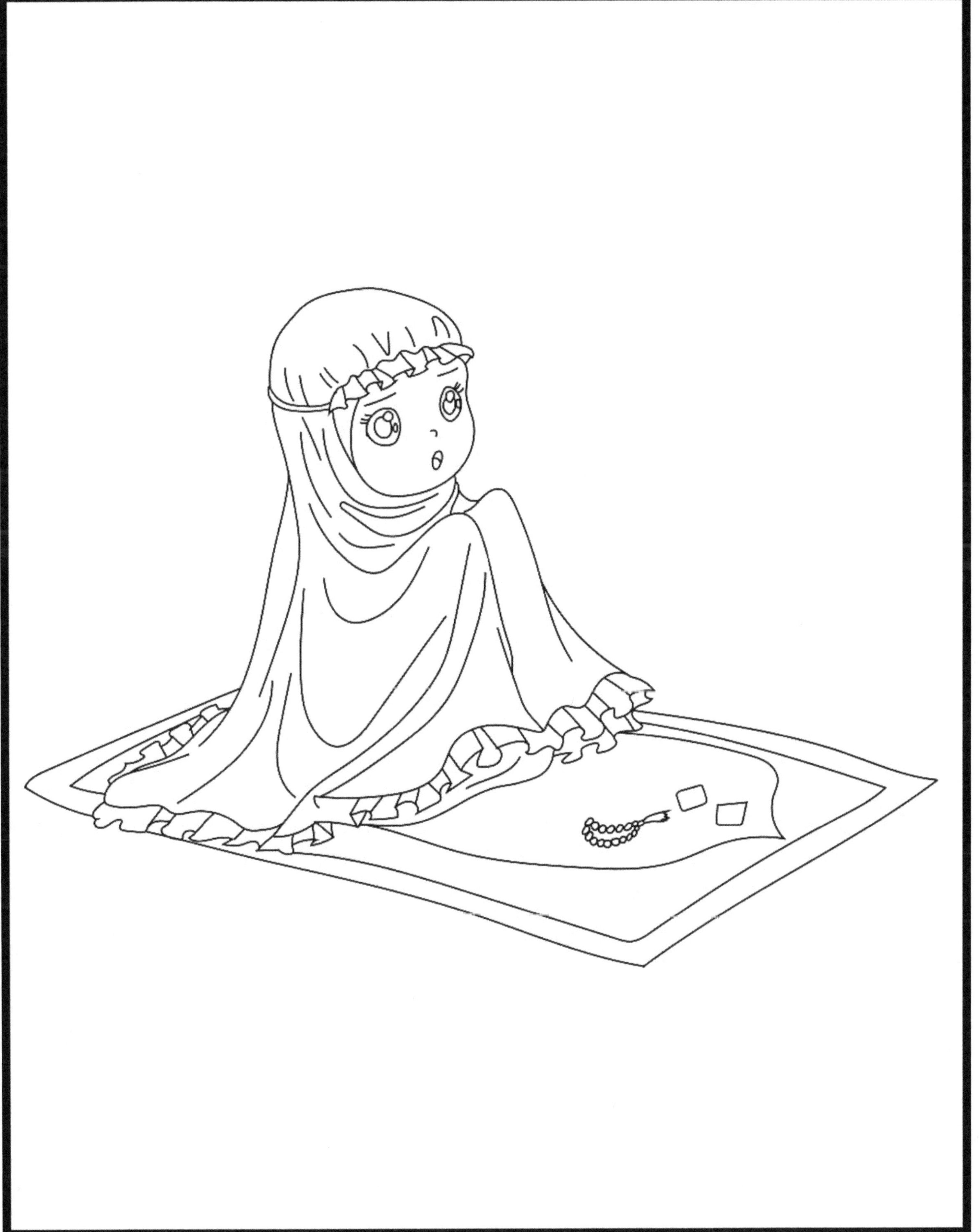

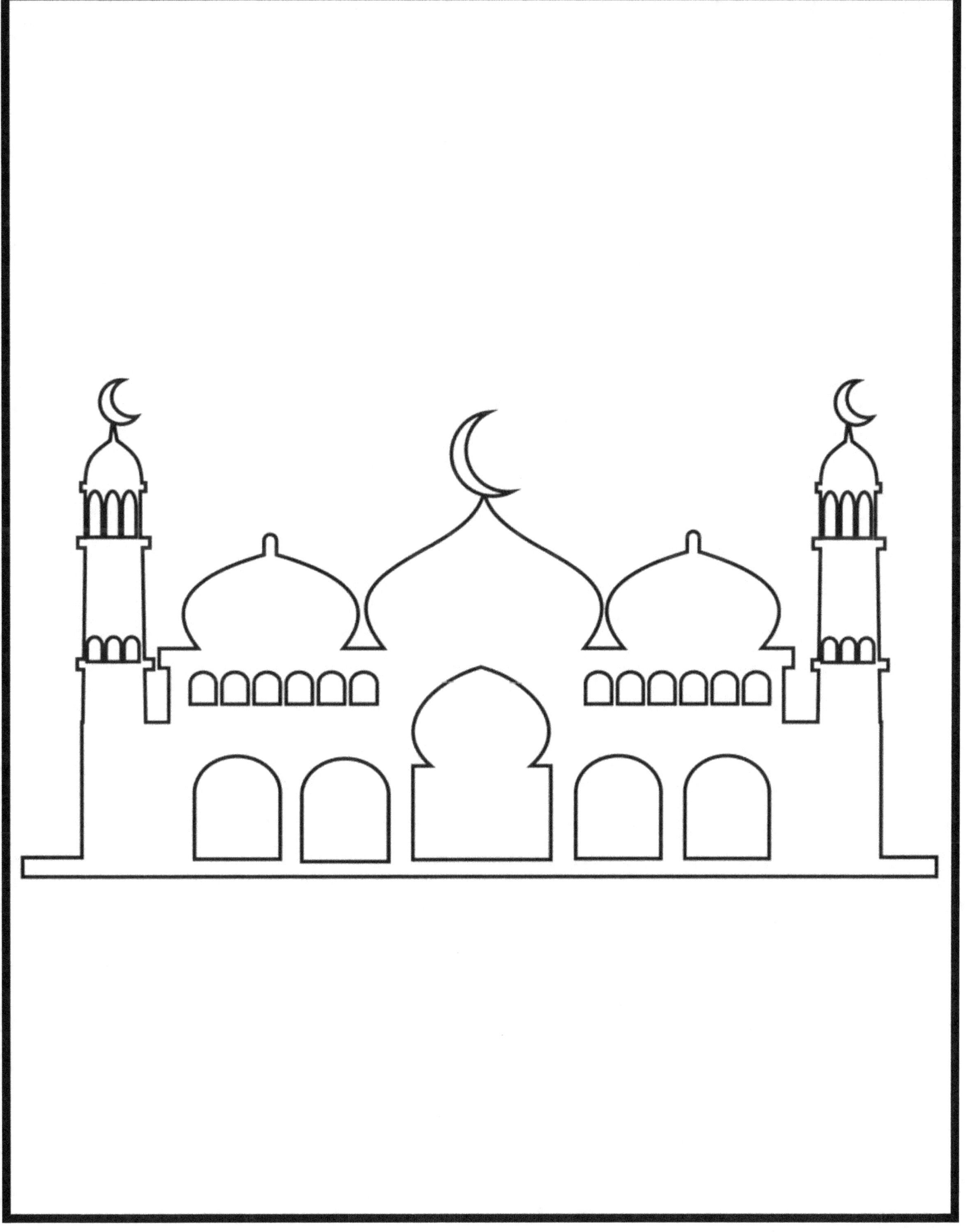

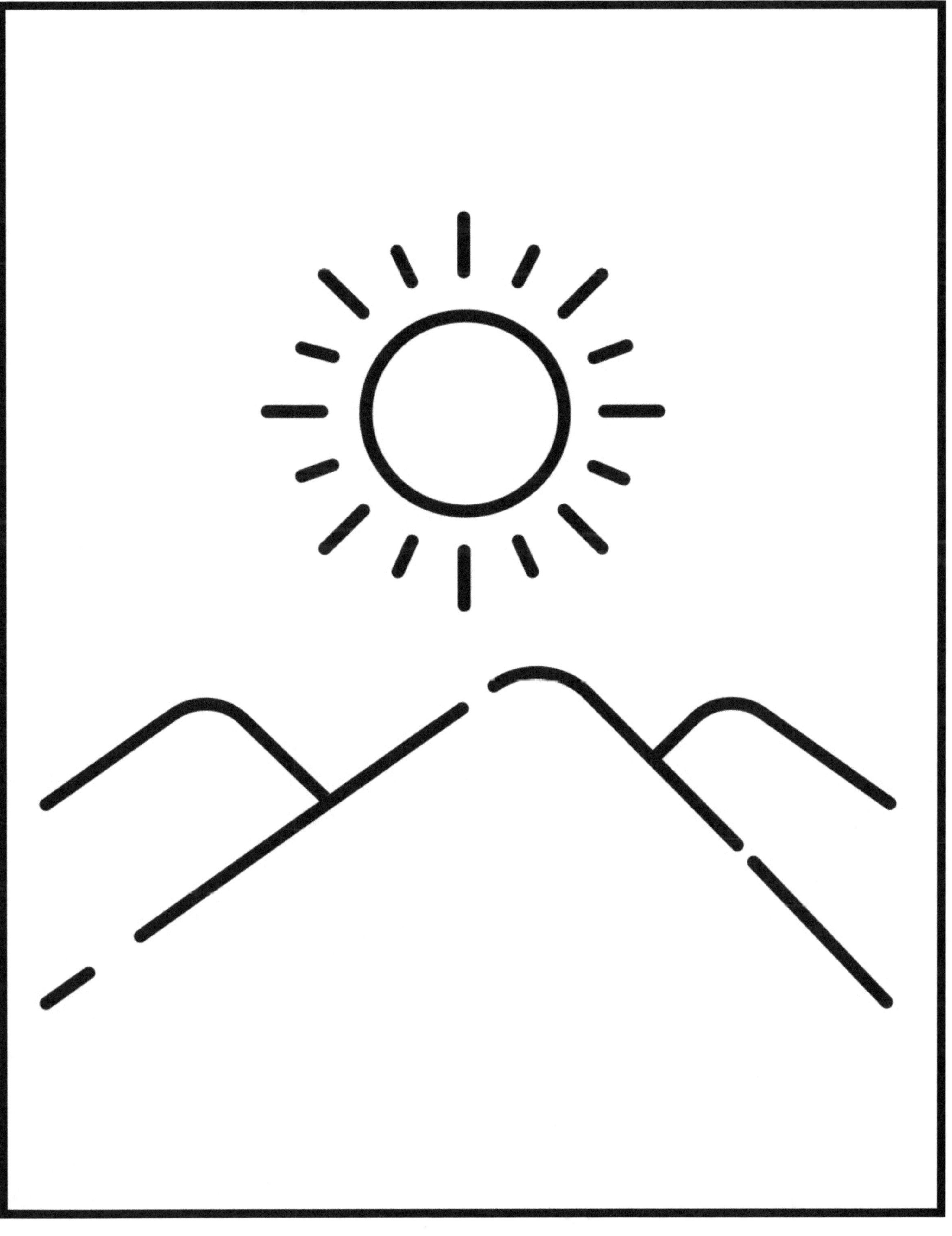

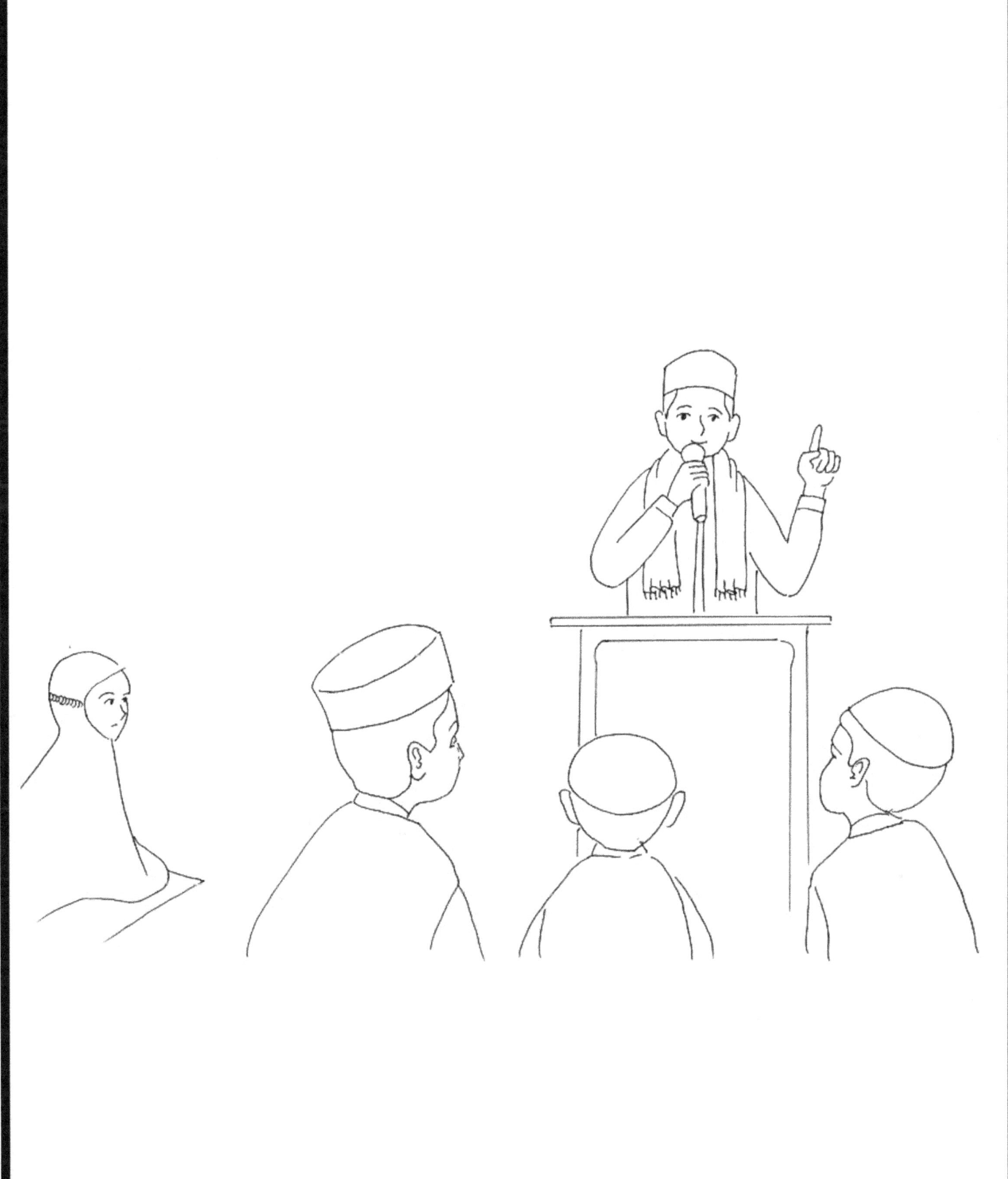

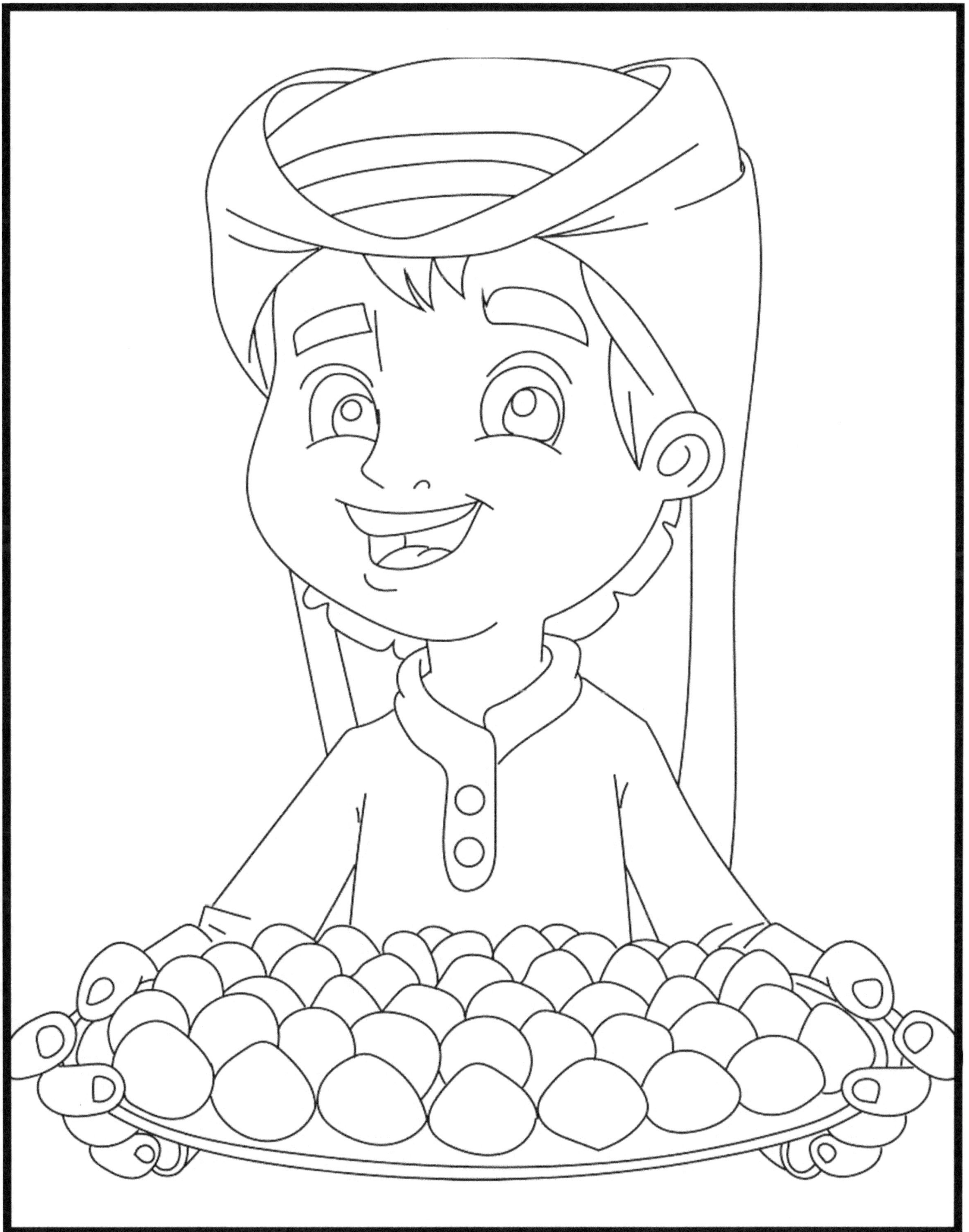

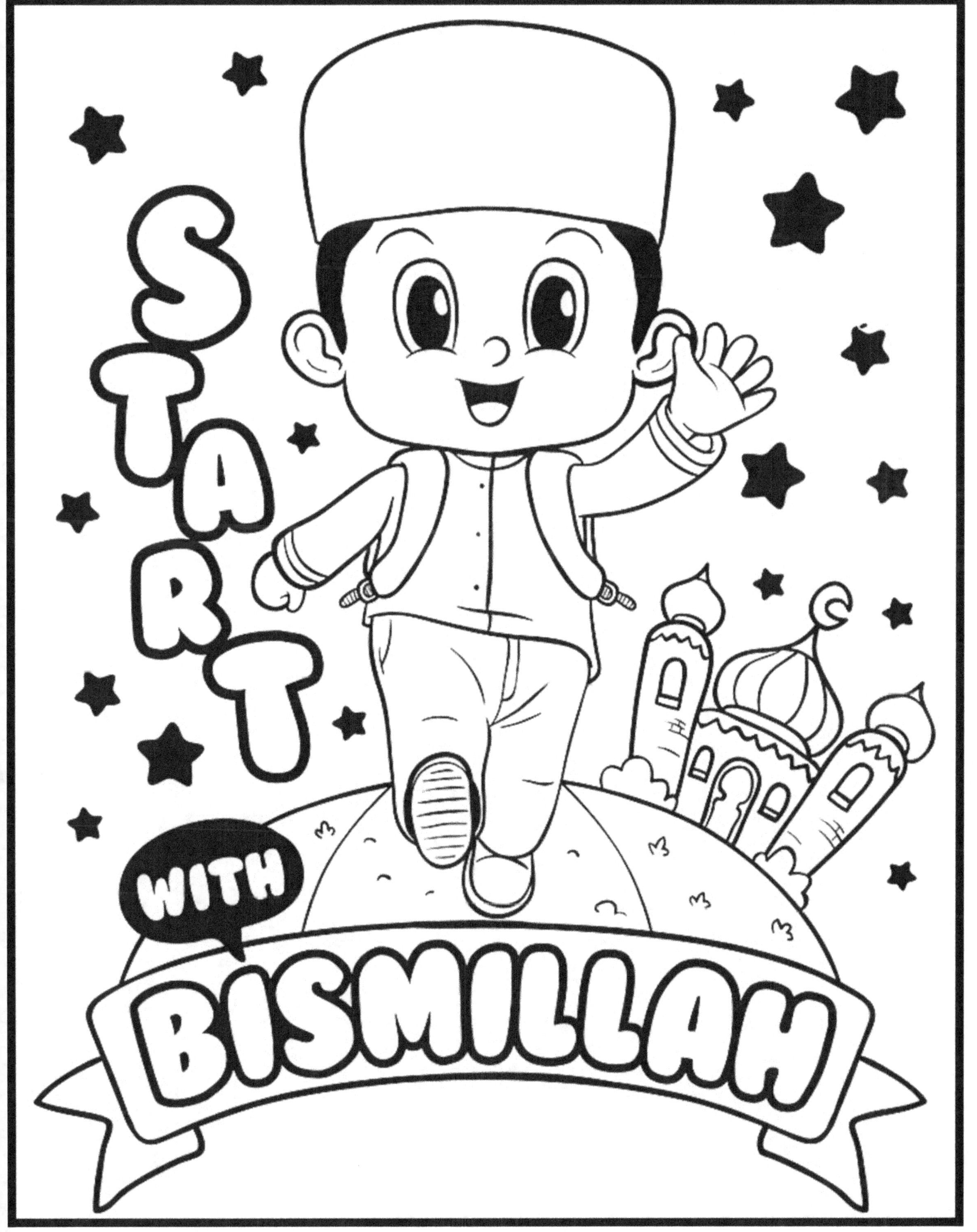

START
WITH
BISMILLAH

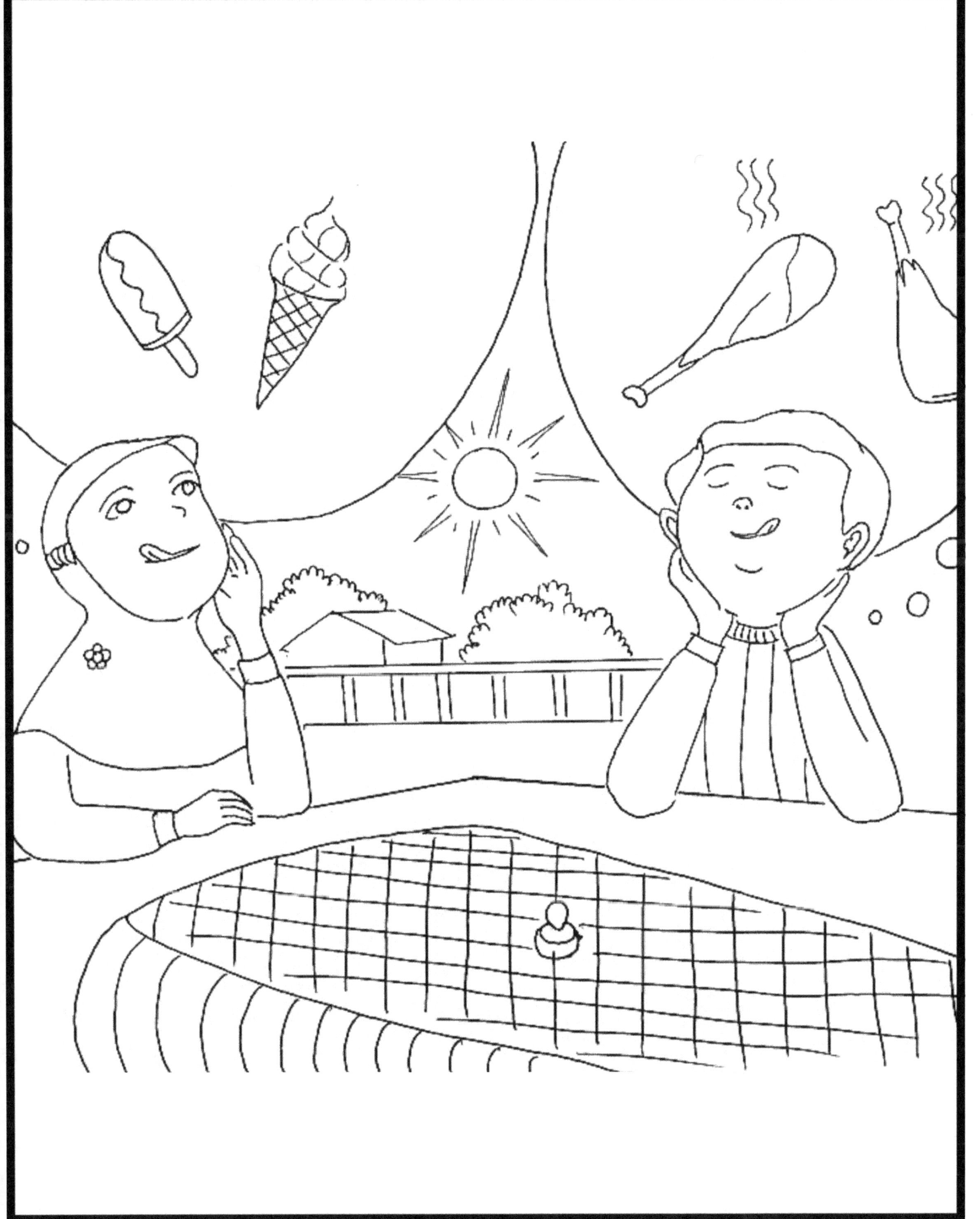

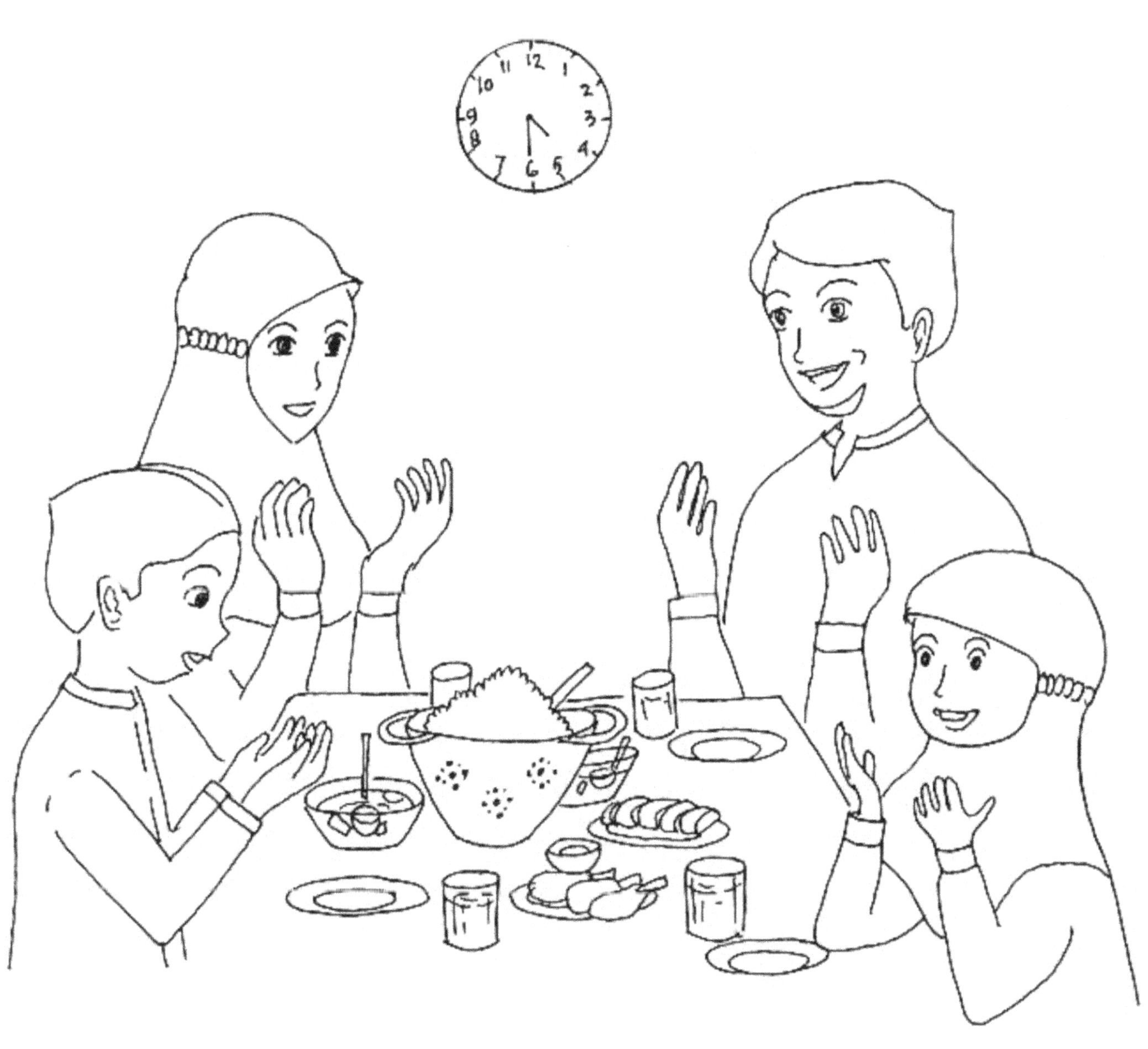

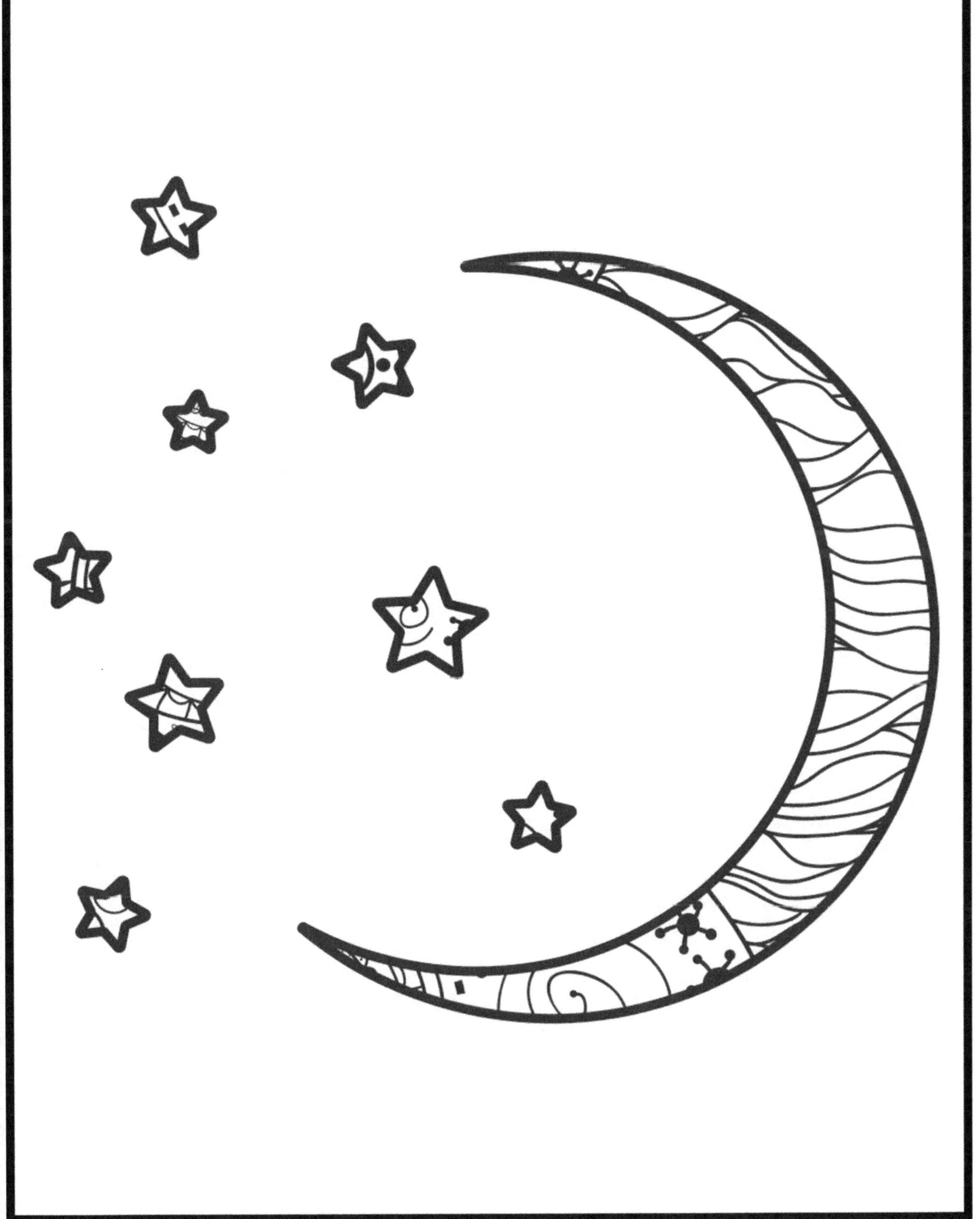

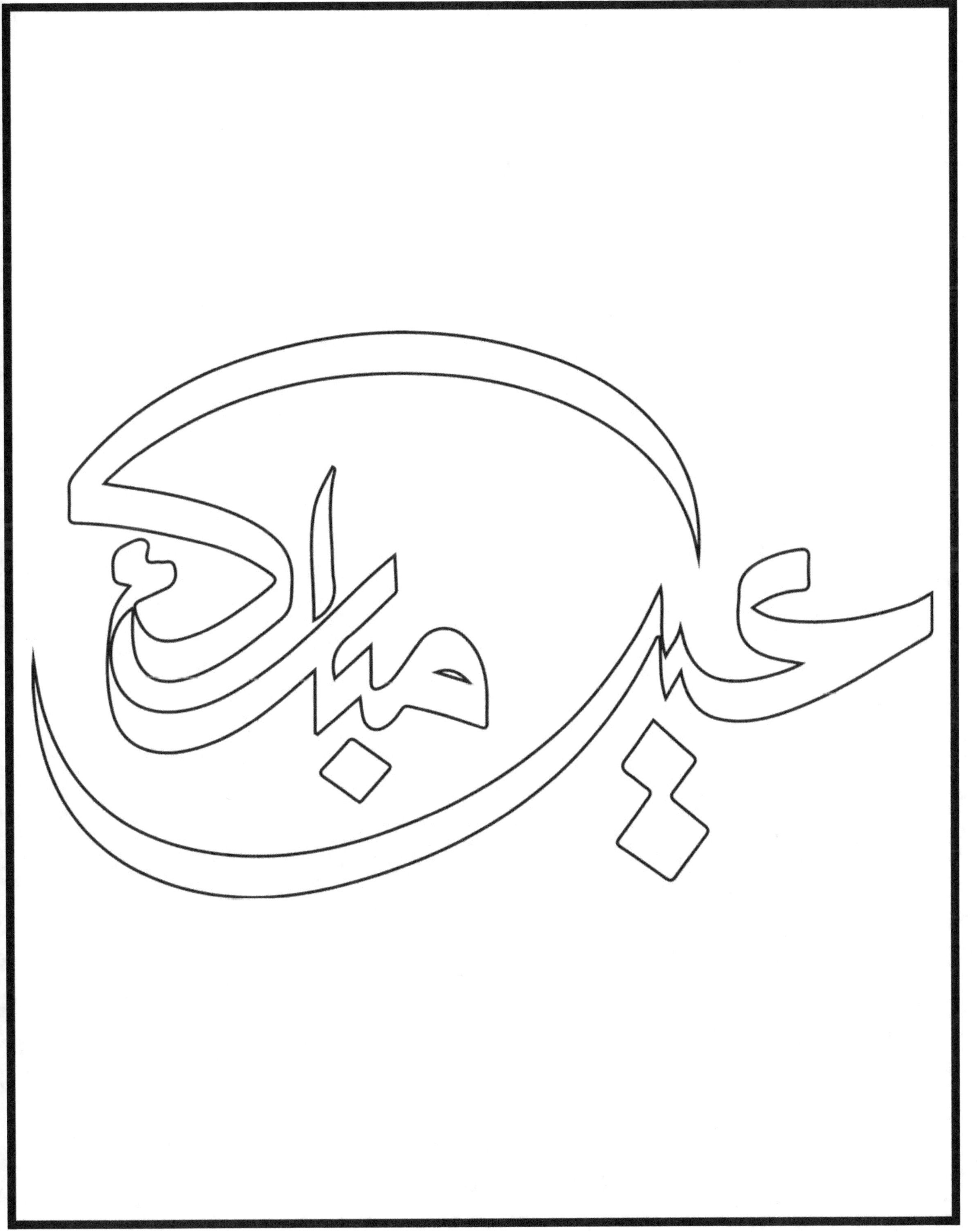
عيد مبارك

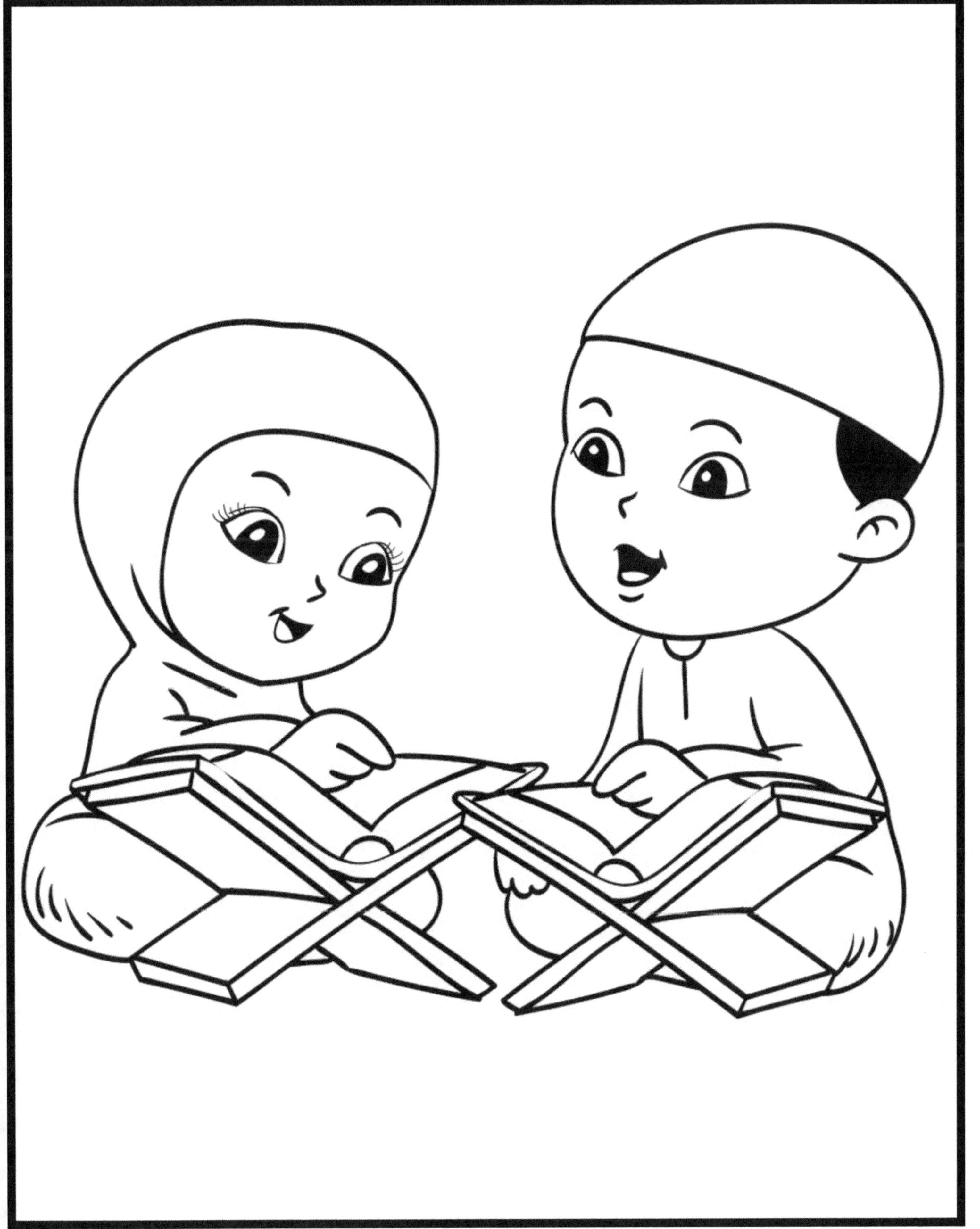

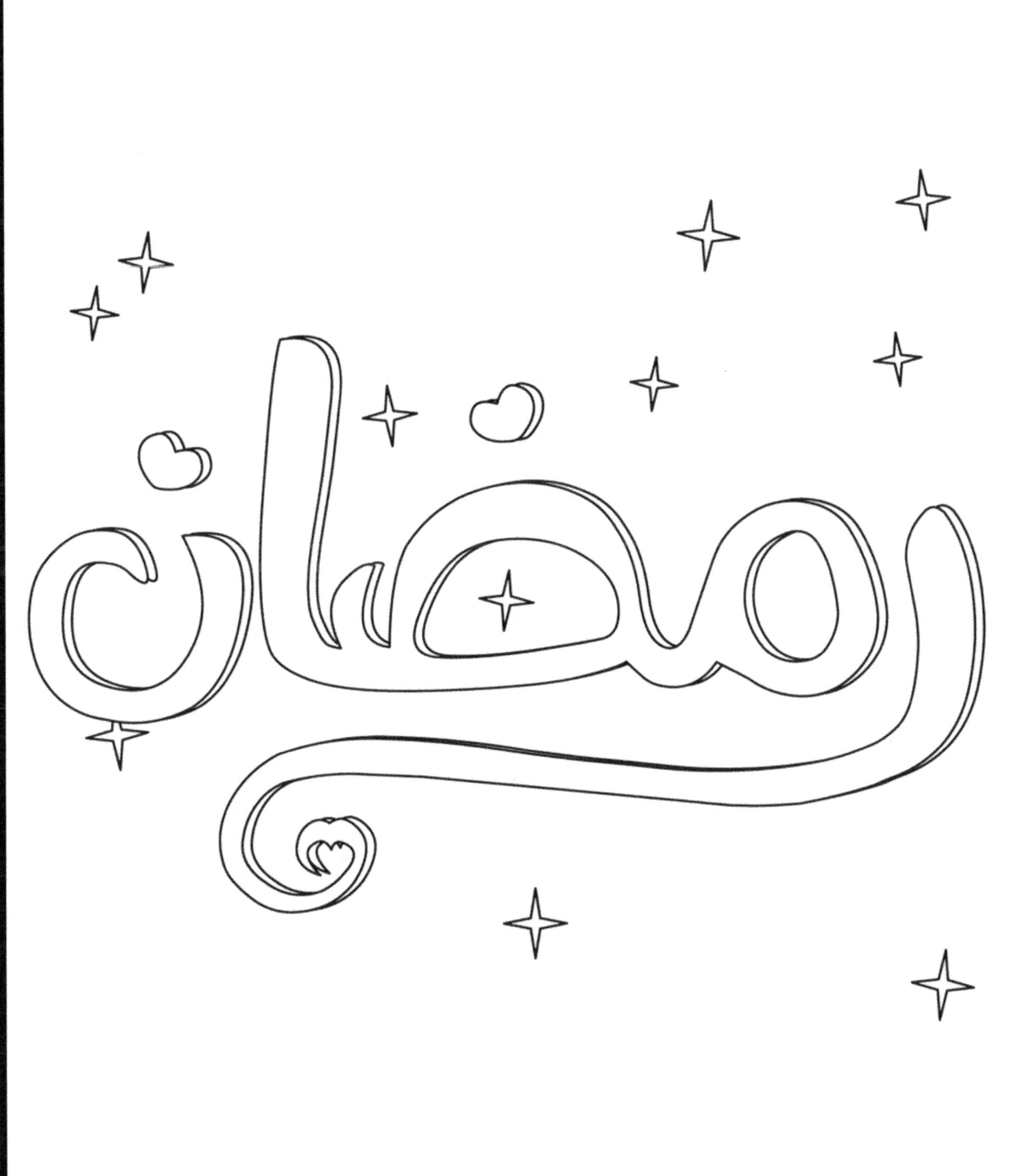

رمضان

Iftar

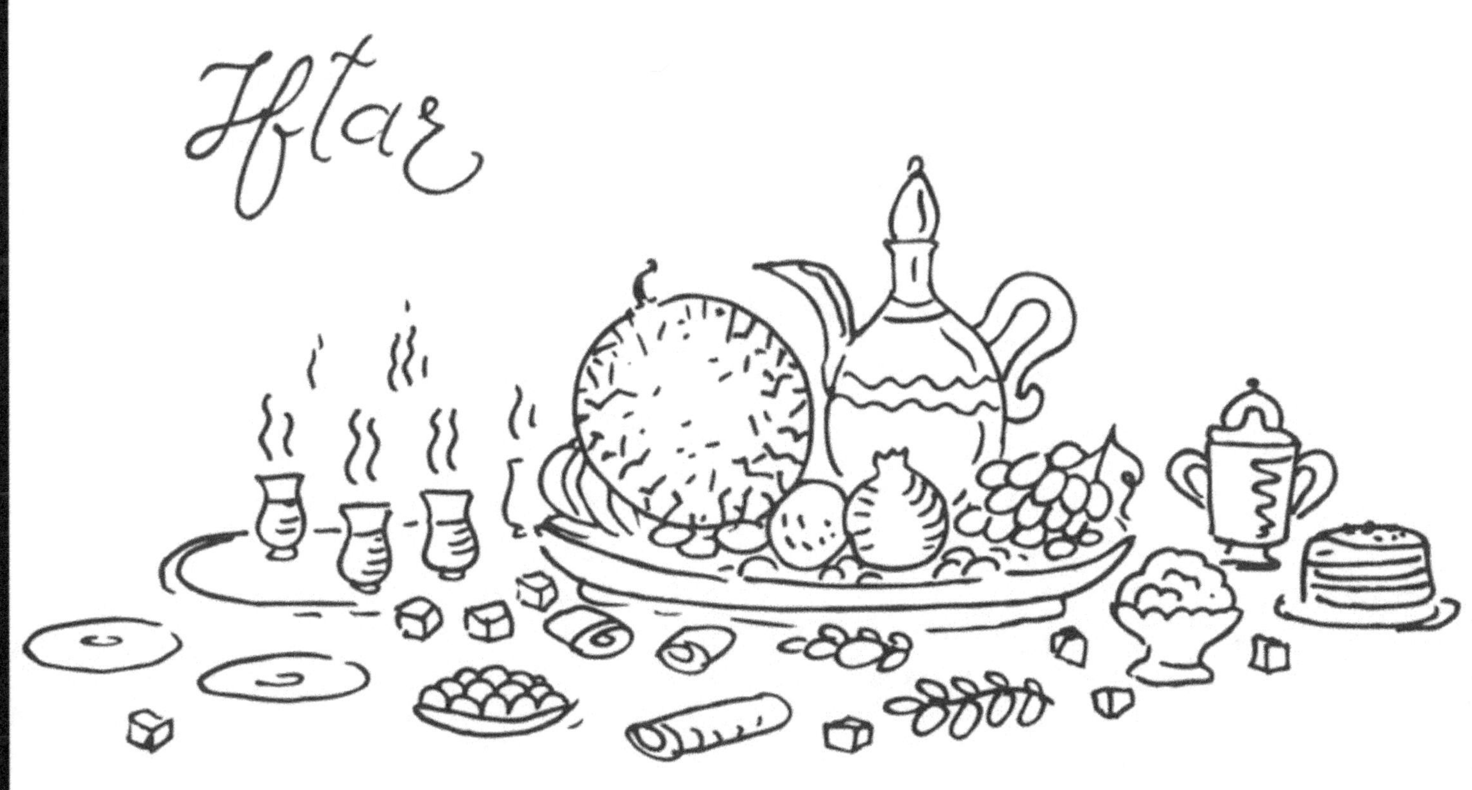

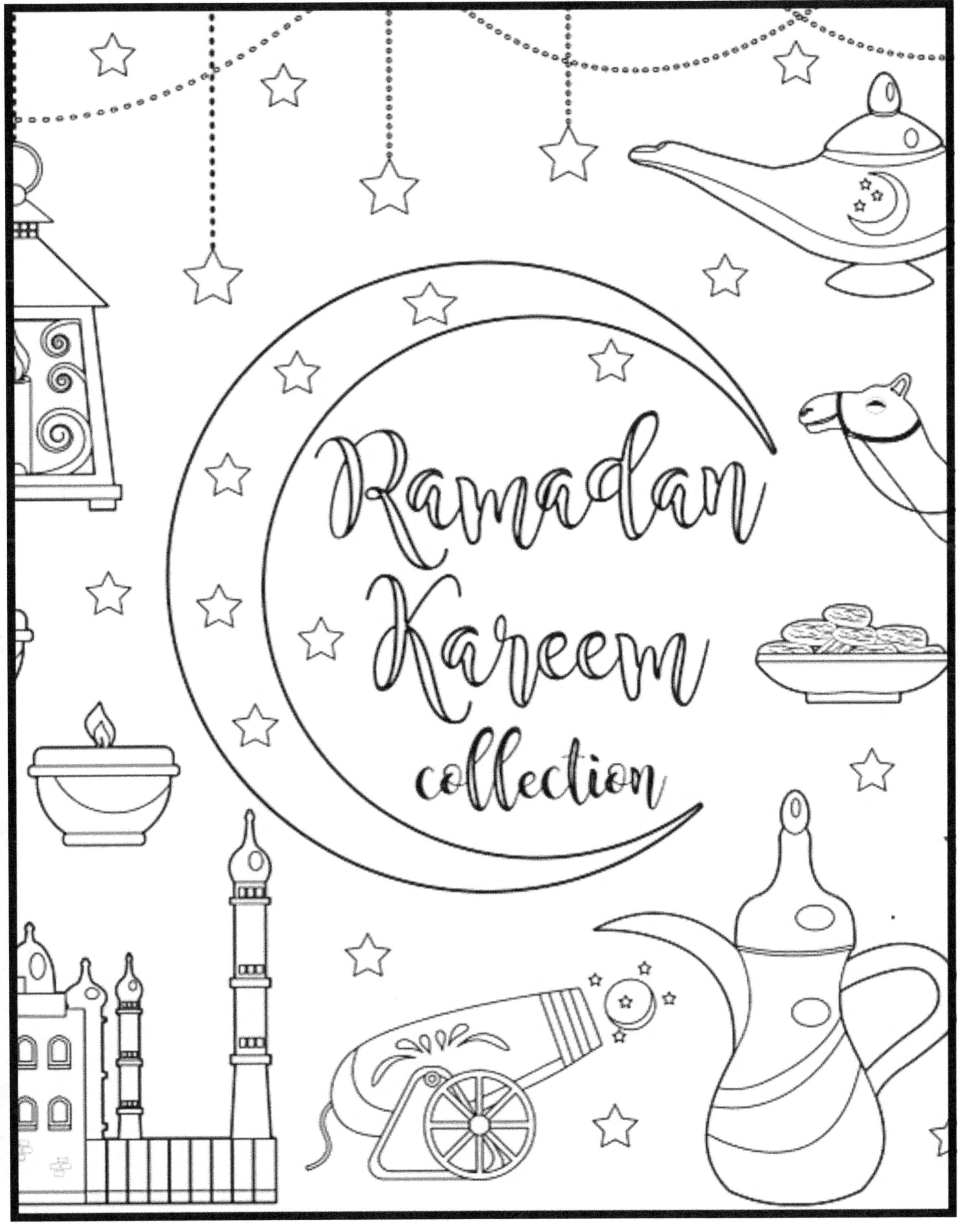
Ramadan
Kareem
collection

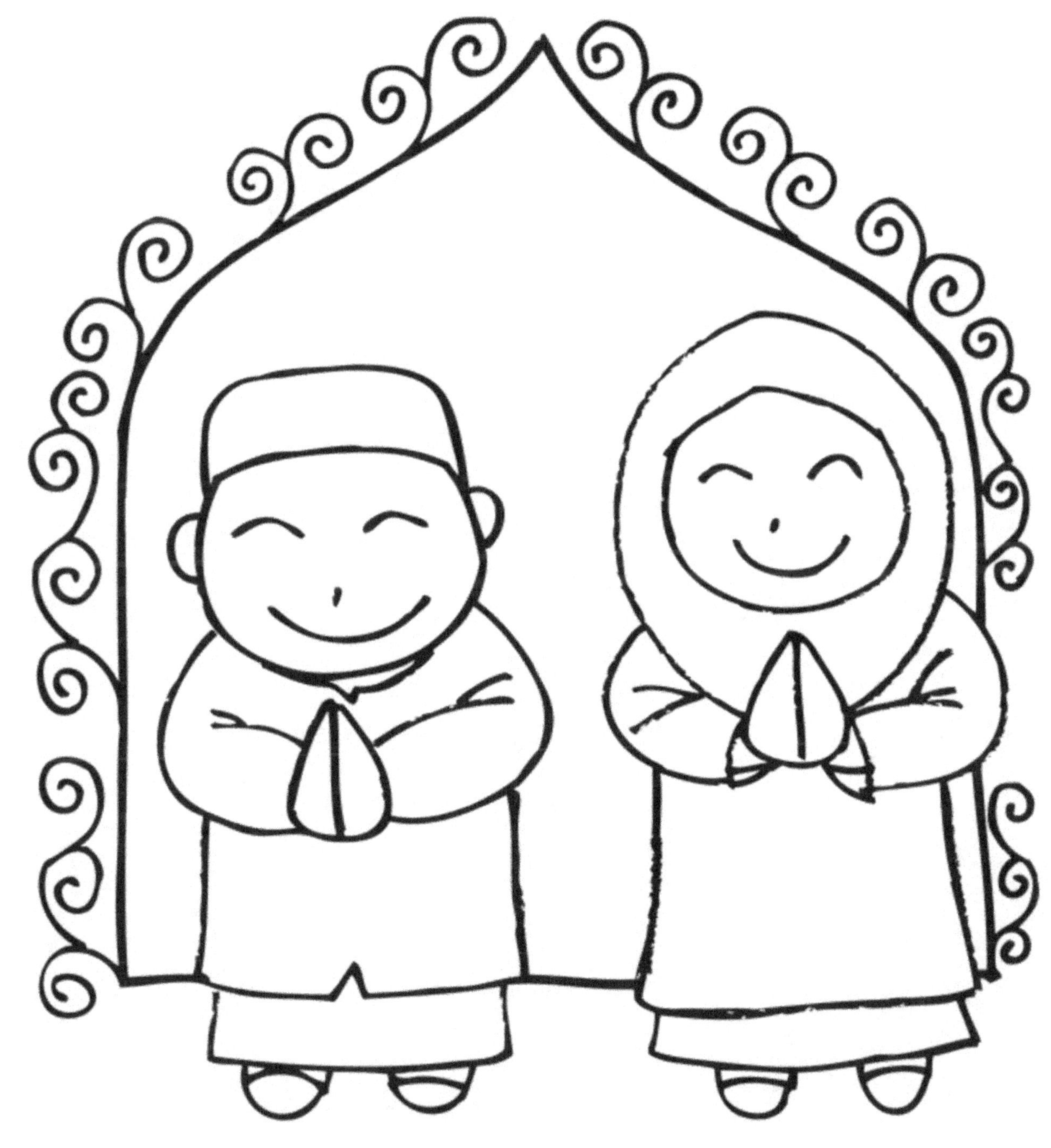

eid mubarak